First published in the United States in 1991 by
Gallery Books, an imprint of W.H. Smith Publishers, Inc.,
112 Madison Avenue, New York, New York 10016
Copyright © 1986 by The Five Mile Prens.
Illustrated by Bob Graham.
Produced by Joshua Morris Publishing, Inc.
in association with The Five Mile Press.
All rights reserved.
Printed in Singapore.
ISBN 0-8317-0932-4

Gallery Books are available for bulk purchase
for sales promotions and premium use. For
details write or telephone the Manager of
Special Sales, W.H. Smith Publishers, Inc.,
112 Madison Avenue, New York, New York 10016,
212/532-6600

Pig's Wild Cart Ride

An early learner book about motion

bob graham

GALLERY BOOKS
An Imprint of W. H. Smith Publishers Inc.
112 Madison Avenue
New York City 10016

Here is Jane with her
cart and her pig.

Jane *pushes* her cart.
This makes it move.

Off we go . . .

...whee...down the hill.

The cart is moving fast.

So is Jane's pig.

Will they ever stop?

The cart keeps on moving until...

...a rock stops the cart.
But the pig is still moving.

What will stop the pig?

The pig slides into a muddy puddle.

The sticky mud stops the pig.
Pigs love mud.

You can start a cart moving
with a push.

Once it is moving…

it keeps on moving...

...until it stops.

moving

Moving objects come to rest, even when no apparent force is applied, because of the force exerted by *gravity* and *friction*. Gravity is the force of attraction that moves bodies toward the center of the earth. Friction is the resistance between two surfaces in contact which are moving one against the other. Friction is reduced by using smooth surfaces and/or providing a lubricant.

Experiments to try
1. Run a metal zipper quickly up and down to gauge the drag caused by friction. Take a black-lead pencil and carefully run the lead along the closed zipper track. Do this a number of times. Now try the zipper again. What has happened? Why? (Graphite in pencil black-lead is a lubricant.)
2. Place a brick on a flat area of concrete. Without jerking, push the brick along the ground to gauge the force required to move it. Now place two or three rollers between the brick and the concrete. (Pencils or dowels will do.) Now push the brick again. What can be observed?